# My Books

# James McQuitty

A James McQuitty Book
Published 1<sup>st</sup> August 2025

Webpage
https://jamesmcquittybooks.mystrikingly.com/

Facebook
https://www.facebook.com/jamesmcquittysharing

YouTube
https://www.youtube.com/@jamesmcquitty8875

# Table of Contents

Foreword ..................................................................................... 5

1. Adventures in Time and Space .................................................. 7

2. Be Yourself .............................................................................. 13

3. Christianity: The Sad and Shameful Truth ............................... 17

4. Escape from Hell ..................................................................... 23

5. Fifty Famous Spirits of the Past Speak ..................................... 33

6. Golden Enlightenment ............................................................ 41

7. Help Yourself to a Better Life .................................................. 47

8. How Psychics and Mediums Work, The Spirit & the Aura ...... 51

9. Immortality ............................................................................. 57

10. Know Thyself, Be Thyself ...................................................... 63

11. Know Yourself ....................................................................... 67

12. My Story ............................................................................... 71

13. Spiritual Astro-Numerology .................................................................. 75

14. The Evolvement of the Soul ................................................................. 79

15. The Great Awakening .......................................................................... 83

16. The Great Awakening-Book Two ......................................................... 91

17. The Reason Why You Were Born ......................................................... 95

18. The Wisdom Oracle .............................................................................. 99

19. The Trilogy ........................................................................................ 103

The Author ............................................................................................... 109

Titles No Longer Available ....................................................................... 110

# 1. Adventures in Time and Space

# Adventures in Time and Space
## The True Story of Who You Really Are
## And Why You Are on Earth

Published February 2015 – Latest Edition July 2025

This is a non-fiction book that contains true information. It is suitable for children (over the age of 11 years is suggested) and adults who seek an understanding of their true nature in time and space.

## About the book

Readers who enjoy sci-fi may think of "Dr Who" when they first see the title of this book. What they may not realise is that, just like Dr Who, they truly are undertaking one of many adventures in time and space.

In the TV series, when 'The Doctor' appears to be dying, the energy that is released **regenerates** back to the physical form creating a new or different body and outward appearance and personality.

In a similar way, when we on Earth complete a physical lifetime (we 'die') we can **reincarnate** through birth into another physical body and develop a personality that may differ from that of the previous physical lifetime.

The book in essence reveals to readers who they really are, and why they are currently on Earth.

To some people this information may seem too incredible to be true; this is because, effectively, people are usually born with amnesia.

Yet, truth can be more amazing than fiction.

So no matter one's age, finding the truths within the pages of this book can be one of the best things that could ever happen to anyone.

# A little from the book

## The Good Adventurer

*Every good adventurer in time and space needs an open mind and a good imagination.*

*They should have a sense of wonderment and be willing to embrace all possibilities.*

*As they explore the universe and many dimensions they should seek to learn from what they discover.*

*It is those who have journeyed long and far and fulfilled such dreams and emerged as wiser beings who can become our guardians and our guides.*

*They are an example to us all.*

## Energy beings enjoy new adventures, surprises and challenges

The spontaneity of Earth life, how we behave and react is a test we energy beings choose to experience; it is the adventure we learn from.

We "test" ourselves to see if we can live and respond to the direction of our true (energy being) self. It may seem a crazy thing to do, to leave our wonderful home world where we have so much freedom and potential to come here and be more limited.

We do so because life in the home world is not a real surprise, in many ways it is too good, and the adventures are not the same as we have on Earth. In the home world we live constantly surrounded by tremendous love, compassion and harmony. We are never too hot or cold, never hungry, never tired, never hurt or injured, we never experience any fear or worry. Yet, it is difficult for us to climb the mountain to higher dimensions without facing challenges.

So as crazy at it may seem we come to Earth to see how we will react to living on a planet that is harsh, and can be unloving and hurtful, to a world where fear rules so many lives. Fear of hunger, of homelessness, of sickness, pain and misery, and a lack of money. We cannot experience these challenges in the home world. And the best way to test the "inner self" is to face some of these challenges with no memory of our true nature and origins.

We come here to see if we can follow our inner self that "speaks" to us via our heart's compassion and the "inner voice" that can be called our "intuition".

Billions of us energy beings accept and choose to return here many, many times in this same state of amnesia.

The reasons why we keep returning to Earth as humans are very clear to us before we return; otherwise we would not keep doing so. It is only here that our past memories are absent.

## More about why you are on Earth

Knowledge comes to us through the experiences of many adventures, with plenty of possible mishaps on the way. Those who are wise use what they learn with kindness, love and compassion.

Being here in physical life gives us the opportunity to experience a vast array of adventures in, as I have said, a completely different form and environment from the home world.

Gradually, it is to be hoped, that these experiences will encourage us to become more knowledgeable and wiser beings.

By the way, the knowledge we energy beings seek isn't any kind of academic or earthly schooling knowledge. In fact, too much concentration upon mere earthly facts and "logic" can be a hindrance to progress. This is because this way of thinking can keep us too focused on the physical and material aspects of life, and this can stop us seeing the whole picture – that we are energy beings from a better world.

The knowledge we energy beings seek is, in a sense, of ourselves. We seek to better "know ourselves", our inner qualities, so that we might better express them. Can we, when on Earth, bring through the kindness, love, compassion and friendship we so naturally express and experience in the home world? This can often prove a difficult test for so many of us.

**Before birth energy beings actually plan their excursions into physical life and formulate what is often called a "Life Plan".**

## Adventures in Time and Space

### Amazon Reviews

### Everyone should read this book - James Aylward, Dec. 2016

'Many who do may not believe it.

'Those who do will increase their trust in life, accept personal responsibility, be less critical of others and help make this world a better place.'

### I recommend it to all seeking proof of life after death - Robert Goodwin, Oct. 2016

'James McQuitty is one of a rare breed - an author possessing real spiritual insight, able to convey his wisdom in ways accessible to everyone through the written word.

'This book combines challenging (to some) information with sound common sense and age old truth.

'I recommend it to all seeking proof of life after death and the knowledge that life is a wonderful journey, leading ultimately to the realisation that we are all one.'

## 2. Be Yourself

# Be Yourself

Published November 2016 – Latest Edition May 2021

### Please note
Part Two of "Know Thyself, Be Thyself"
Includes this manuscript

### About the book

This book shares some of my observations and thoughts of how we might better be true to our inner self.

In this, I am sure readers will find much to consider. In places they may even find it amusing?

However, more seriously, readers may, perhaps, also find some inspiration to encourage them to make some positive changes in how they approach life and interact with family, friends and other people?

At least the book may give them some 'food for thought'.

Naturally, we are all free spirits at all times, so the final decisions we make on absolutely everything in life are our own to make.

Most people, it seems to me, think that they are already living exactly how they choose?

But many people are not.

They are pushed and pulled, manipulated or coerced in various ways to behave and live in ways that do not reflect their real true inner self.

The flock mentality inhibits many people from thinking freely for themselves; consequentially, they behave and respond according to the dictates of their "programming".

Some programming is of course very, very difficult to overcome; and this is especially so if it originated in childhood.

Surely though, true freethinkers ought to apply the results of their free thinking to absolutely everything that they say, do, and even think?

## A Little from the Book

### From Section 5 on "Comedians"

Many sheepish people have their "adopted shepherds". In some cases this includes comedians who appear in theatres or on TV.

The comedian may say something which is "funny", for instance, about spirits, ghosts or the afterlife; or derogatory about mediums. What they say will get a laugh, and suddenly the subject and all who work in this field are to some easily led people fit only for ridicule.

If this stayed within the confines of a theatre or TV comedy routine this would, perhaps, be of lesser concern. However, it doesn't; it gets into the collective psyche of many of the gullible sheepish members of society. Consequently, they assume that all mediums, including the most honourable and genuine, are frauds or deluded individuals.

Anyone who dares to utter a word in defence of the accused people or subject is laughed at by all in the flock. The little voice in the head may say, "But I know there are genuine mediums and life beyond the physical", but this is kept quiet because freethinking is not permitted in the flock. They feel that they must, "follow the pathway of obedience or be ostracised".

## From Section 10 on "The Government"

The bottom line in this section is to encourage readers to recognise that they are equal members of the human race whilst on Earth. We are all entitled to an opinion, and should have the right to expect a truly decent person to be elected to represent the community in which we live.

We need to see beyond the facade that allows others to dominate national and world policies. Are such people serving us, have they the good of all at heart? Or are they behaving outside of moral if not literal legal limits for their own personal agenda, profit and power? I think the latter is all too often the case.

2021 Update: In fact, at present as I type this it seems those who are directing life in the UK and in many countries globally are behaving like social-psychopaths who are 'hell bent' on destroying the livelihood and natural health of their citizens. It seems they have 'overnight' signed-up to an agenda to 'jab' every person they possibly can for no genuine and truthful good reason. They probably believe they will face no consequences, despite the fact that what they are doing has, in my opinion, nothing to do with health and could even lead to a mass reduction in the world population. They, it seems, have no concept or belief or understanding in an 'afterlife' and natural laws and the karma they are sowing. This, I feel, will certainly propel some of these people to a very, very dark realm of spirit life.

# 3. Christianity: The Sad and Shameful Truth

# Christianity: The Sad and Shameful Truth

Published March 2014 – Latest Edition March 2024

## About the book

I must first say that I am not in any sense an 'academic religious scholar' who has devoted decades of his life to the subject of Christianity or religion.

So those readers who want every "i" dotted and every "t" crossed and to find material written in a way that suggests 'academia', or for that matter some new 'revelation' derived from some ancient manuscript, should look elsewhere.

What I am, is a sensible individual who even as a child had the commonsense to never for one second fall for the 'crazy' zealous and guilt ridden teachings of the Christian Church.

In this book readers will find plenty of simple and easy to read explanations of the origins of Christianity, and the sad and shameful truth of how over its history it has directly or indirectly abused billions of people.

Read this book if you dare.

## A Little from pages 35-38 of the Book

- 'If a man has a stubborn and rebellious son who will not obey his father or mother' the Bible instructs that they should be "stoned to death", and that 'everyone should hear of this and fear'. (Deuteronomy c.21 v.18-21)
- 'Happy is he who repays you for what you have done to us by seizing your infants and dashing them against the rocks'. (Psalm c.137 v.9)
- 'With a great plague will the LORD smite your people and children, and your wives. You shall have great sickness

*by disease of your bowels, until they fall out'. (2 Chronicles c.21 v.14-15)*

If any Christian today is truly gullible enough to totally accept Bible teachings, they should ask themselves why the laws of Christian countries do not reflect what it says. The answer is because any person with an ounce of commonsense, reason or fair judgment realises that the Bible does not reflect the total truth of history, or of how life should be led, no more than it reflects the true laws or teachings of God.

The story of Noah's ark, as told by Moses in Genesis, is a fantasy that totally lacks commonsense.

In this crazy fictitious story God (supposedly) saw that the wickedness of people on Earth had grown so great with every thought evil that he said:

- *'I will destroy man (and women and animals, etc.) whom I have created from the face of the Earth'. (Genesis c.6 v.5-8)*

However, and 'somehow':

- *'Noah found grace in the eyes of the Lord (God)'. (Genesis C.6 v.5-8)*

According to the Bible, God then proceeded to instruct Noah to build an ark, and gave instructions as to its material and size, telling Noah that he and his wife, three sons, and their wives, and "two of every living thing", along with adequate provisions, should be taken on board the ark. Although in later instructions, at the start of chapter seven, some, such as fowls, were increased in numbers to seven. Are we to assume God made a mistake in his original instructions?

Furthermore, it does not say just how Noah was to accomplish this totally and utterly impossible task. There is no mention of him travelling the entire world in order to gather this 'two of every living thing'. There are millions of different species of animals alone!! Did the instruction include insects?

How about plants, because these too are 'living things'? One might also ask, with the 'provisions' he was to take, 'did he take spare animals' for those animals who are carnivorous to feed upon? Also, did he take various types of non-carnivore feed to cater not only for all the other diverse forms of animal life but to satisfy the animals the carnivores were later to feed upon?

Then one might ask, 'was this ark divided into separate isolation sections (or cages)' like in a zoo? Surely this would have been the only way possible to prevent all the different animals from attacking and in some cases eating each other?

If we also take a closer look at the size of this fictional ark. It was said to be 300 x 50 x 30 cubits in size. This is approximately a maximum size in feet of 520 long x 87 wide x 52 high. These days the number of different animal species in the world is estimated to be 8.7 million in total!!! Even if we were to 'imagine' there were only one-tenth of this number at the time of Noah, and there may well have been more, would these have had even the slightest chance of fitting in the supposed available space? **No they would not!!!**

It is all such utter nonsense.

During the floods which reportedly followed, Noah reached six hundred years of age. After some one hundred and fifty days afloat, all life upon Earth other than in the ark was destroyed.

At the end of the story, when the land was dry, and all had disembarked from the ark, we are told that God then instructed Noah and his sons to begin repopulating the Earth.

- *'God blessed Noah and his sons,' and said, 'be fruitful, and multiply, and replenish the Earth'. (Genesis c.9 v.1)*

This is obviously stating that God encouraged a vast amount of very close breeding, and perhaps even incest, to replenish the Earth. In the same manner incest would have been the only way the human race could have got started if we were to believe in the Bible story of Adam and Eve, as told in Genesis. How very unpleasant the thought is.

It also says that after the flood Noah lived another three-hundred-and-fifty years, and did not pass until he was nine-hundred-and-fifty years old!!

If any Christian is gullible enough to actually believe that the story of Noah's ark is a true one I will be amazed!

The story teaches that God destroyed all men, women, children, newly born babies, pregnant mothers to be, the old and infirm, the blind, and the crippled and practically every innocent animal.

I ask, does this really sound like a just and forgiving God, one who also tells us to "love our enemies"? The whole episode, as with so much of the Bible, is full of contradiction, fabrication and fantasy in an attempt to favour those who wished to dominate others.

It is an example of how the Bible has and is sometimes still used to keep Christians in fear of a revengeful and cruel God.

Another point Christians are unable to answer concerns the age of Noah. If we were to believe the Bible, we would have to accept the amazing longevity of Noah. Why did he live so long? And did he have other wives whom he outlived before the one at the time of the flood? Then, we might ask, what about all the years between his reported age of six hundred at the time of the flood and his passing at the age of nine hundred and fifty years. Did his wife live to be as old as he? Then what are we to make of his three sons and their wives. Were the sons the product of Noah's most recent marriage at the time of the flood, and did he have other families whom he had outlived? Did he ignore and leave to drown all the grandchildren and great grandchildren from previous marriages? Or are we to assume that Noah waited until he was well into his five-hundreds before he married and had his only three sons? Or were the three sons and their wives also hundreds of years old?

Surely this would have made the repopulating of the world a tiring, if not biologically impossible task for them all?

**Christianity: The Sad and Shameful Truth**

Amazon Review

Finally! – Summy, May 2025

*'Finally someone had that courage to speak this truth. This book is succinct and to the point in revealing in a simple, no-nonsense, and often hilarious manner, the many absurdities, atrocities, and contradictions in the Bible and the Christian church. I have cross referenced James' Bible references, and agree whole heartedly with his perspectives. Fantastic book for any recovering born again Christian like myself.'*

# 4. Escape from Hell

# Escape from Hell

Published February 2019 – Latest Edition August 2021

## About the book

Escape from Hell is a story of eternal hope. It is a 'fictionalized' story that is based upon communications direct from the spirit world which, in 1896, were recorded in *'A Wanderer in the Spirit Lands'*. One advantage of this shorter and easier to read book is that it benefits from highly informative **"Corroborative Evidence"** that supplies readers with plenty of material and recommendations of where to find further reading material and other valuable evidence.

The main character in the story is, "Antonio". It is his account of what transpired when he 'died', or rather, his physical body died.

It takes us right from the very first 'after death' circumstances he faced, to how he was guided and helped, and through his own efforts helped himself, and gradually began to climb the spiritual ladder to, "Escape from Hell".

Antonio gives us examples of what can, and for all too many people does, for them follow their Earth life. It shows us how those people who have lived solely for themselves, or morally corrupt, cruel, unjust, harmful, unforgiving, and destructive or in any way evil lives, find they have for themselves created nothing but miserable circumstances awaiting them when they first depart Earth life.

Antonio also tells us how, inspired and motivated by his genuine love for Angelica, a beautiful soul still on Earth, he was gradually able to progress from darkness and misery to brighter and happier regions of spirit life - from darkness into light.

So often, it is only the "brighter and happier regions of spirit life" that we hear about. Thousands of messages to this effect are relayed every week by mediums in Spiritualist demonstrations and services, and at independent venues as well as during private sittings. Loved ones communicate to reassure those on Earth that life is eternal, and that they are happy in the "afterlife" as it is so often called.

Such communications tell us of happy reunions with family and friends, with animals too, and of the beautiful conditions in which they live and await us when "our time comes".

All this is fine and correct, assuming one has led a reasonably decent and good life, having been a caring and sharing and in one way or another kind, compassionate and even a mere 'reasonably loving' kind of person.

**However we on Earth should be aware that the simple fact of believing in "life after death" guarantees us nothing.**

It certainly does not ensure one's transition to a higher and brighter spirit realm.

Many people say they believe in an afterlife and still live and behave in ways unbecoming to an evolved soul, to say the least.

Readers of this book will therefore discover the initial fate of those who, when on Earth, lived the worst kind of lives. But they will also see how such souls can be helped, and how they can progress, and that progress is eternally possible. That no one is eternally damned or condemned, and that there is hope for all, even the most degraded of souls.

# A Little from the Book

## Chapter Thirteen: The Fires of Hell

The pathway I was next inspired to follow led me to the entrance to a vast cave. Like so much in this realm it was truly more horrible than mere words can convey. Giant funguses and hideous slim covered plants hung from the roof, and a dark pool of stagnant water covered much of the floor.

When I turned a corner in this cave I saw before me flames coming from an open fire. Dancing around the fire were dark spirits who, in appearance, looked more like evil goblins from some fictional horror story, yet they were real. They had at one time been people on Earth, but as I had personally found, as a spirit is, the form in spirit life becomes in its outward appearance.

**I knew that I was invisible to these beings; this allowing me to observe what they were doing without fear of attack. To my horror I realised that the fire was composed of the bodies of living spirits who wriggled and thrashed about in the flames.**

I was so appalled by this discovery that I called out to higher brothers to find out whether what I could see was a real scene, or only some horrible illusion of this dreadful place. The reply I received told me that those in the flames were living souls who, in their earthly lives, had themselves doomed hundreds of people to die in this same dreadful way. They had shown their victims no pity in doing so, and, they still had developed no remorse.

**Their own cruelties were what had kindled these fierce flames. I had already learned that in the spirit world what we think in our hearts so often becomes an objective reality. So the fires were being generated by the cruelties inflicted by these people upon others when they were**

upon Earth. I could also see that there was not one ounce of pain or anguish they now suffered that had not been suffered a hundredfold more by their helpless victims. Many of whom had now become the revengeful torturers.

I was told that from the fire the spirits would emerge touched by a pity for those they had wronged in the past. Then they could be helped and encouraged to take the path of progression, through deeds of mercy, as many and as great as had been their merciless deeds in the past.

I learned that such retribution as this is allowed because the souls of spirits such as these are so hard, so cruel, that only sufferings felt by themselves could make them pity others. Furthermore, that ever since they had left the Earth life, they had been making others more helpless suffer until, finally, their bitter hatred had drawn them down to this dark cave and engulfed them in the fires.

I was also reminded that the flames I witnessed were not really material, although they appeared to be.

As I watched the flames began to die back until finally they were fully extinguished, then, much to my surprise, from the fire the souls that had occupied it began to emerge. One of whom I was told to follow. As I did so I saw that spirit, with the newly awakened thought of repentance, returning to a city to warn others of his kind, and to try to turn them from the path of his own wrong doings. He did not yet realise the length of time that had elapsed since he had left the Earth life, nor that this city to which he went was the spiritual counterpart of the one he had lived in on Earth.

In time, I was told, he would be sent back to Earth to work as a spirit in helping to teach mortals the pity and mercy he had not shown in his own life. But first he would have to work here in this dark place, striving to release the souls of those whom his torturous crimes had drawn down with him. He had drawn them down because he had driven them to breaking point where all that consumed them was a desire for revenge. These were once decent innocent people who were now filled with burning hatred.

While I stood watching this spirit, I saw pass before me a panorama of his life.

**I saw him first as leader of his order, sitting as a judge before whom were brought many poor Inca Indians and heretics, as he deemed them to be, and I saw him condemning them by hundreds to torture and to be thrown into one of many burning fires because they would not become converts to his teachings. I saw him oppressing all who were not powerful enough to resist him, and extorting jewels and gold in enormous quantities as tribute to him and to his order; and if any sought to resist him and his demands he had them arrested and almost without even the pretence of a trial thrown into dungeons and tortured or burned.**

**I read in his heart existed an absolute thirst for wealth and power and an actual love for witnessing the sufferings of his victims. I knew, reading as I seemed to do his innermost soul that his religion was but a cloak, a convenient name, under which to extort the gold he loved and to enable him to gratify his lust for power.**

I saw a great square within this city with hundreds of great fires blazing all round it until it was like a furnace, and a whole helpless crowd of timid gentle natives were bound hand and foot and thrown into the flames. Their cries of agony went up to the spirit world as this cruel man and his vile accomplices chanted their false prayers, and held aloft an ornate golden cross.

I saw that this horror was perpetrated in the name of the Catholic Church, and of Jesus, whose teachings were of love. Yet this man had no thought of love or pity for these helpless victims. All he thought of was how the spectacle would strike terror into the hearts of other Indian tribes, and make them bring him more gold to satisfy his lust for riches.

Then I saw that this man had returned to his own country and how he had revelled in his ill-gotten wealth. How he had been celebrated as a great and holy man the people believed had gone out to other lands to preach the gospel of love and peace. While, instead, his path had been marked in fire and blood.

**Then I saw this man upon his deathbed, and I saw monks and priests chanting mass for his soul that it might go to Heaven, and instead I saw it drawn down and down to Hell by the chains woven in his wicked life.**

**I saw the great hordes of his former victims awaiting him there, drawn down in their turn by their thirst for revenge, their hunger for power to avenge their sufferings and the sufferings of those most dear to them.**

I saw this man in Hell surrounded by those he had wronged, and in Hell the only thought of that spirit was rage because his power on Earth was no more. His only idea was how he might join with others in Hell as cruel as himself, and even there still oppress and torture.

If he could have doomed his victims to death a second time he would have done so. In his heart then there was neither pity nor remorse, only anger that he was so powerless.

Had he possessed one feeling of sorrow or one thought of kindness for another, it would have helped him. As it was, his passion for cruelty was so great it had fed the spiritual flames.

Those spirits I had beheld, who looked like demons, were the last and most fierce of his victims in whom the desire for revenge was even then not fully satisfied.

**I then saw this Inca city as it had been on Earth before the invasion and Inquisition had arrived. I saw a peaceful**

gentle people living upon fruits and grains and leading their simple lives in an innocence akin to that of childhood. They had worshipped the Great Spirit under a name of their own with greater understanding in spirit laws and truths than those who invaded and claimed their faith superior. Their simple faith and their virtues truly were the outcome of inspiration given to them from the spirit world.

Then I saw their invaders arrive, thirsting for gold, and greedy to grasp the goods of others. Yet these simple people welcomed them like brothers, and in their innocence showed them the treasures they had gathered from the Earth, gold and silver and jewels.

Then I saw the treachery, and how they plundered and killed the simple natives. How all promises were broken, and then the tortures and slavery began, forcing them to labour in the mines until they died by the thousands. The peaceful happy country becoming filled with blood and misery.

I then left this man to begin working on his own redemption.

Corroborative Evidence of Lower, Darker Spirit Realms

An older book (first published 1961) that I very much enjoyed reading by another out-of-body explorer is titled, Excursions to the Spirit World by Frederick C. Sculthorp; here are some examples (2 to 6) from his book in which readers may draw parallels with what Antonio says.

2. The Plane of Illusion

When I arrived on a lower plane I would at once know the nature of the place. The spirit body is very sensitive and at once picks up the thoughts of the people there. The result is a sickening harshness which is indescribable. The most depressing moments on Earth cannot compare with it, as the physical mind cannot deal with many thoughts at a time, whereas the spirit body is open to the mass thought of that particular state.

However, if I had to stay awhile to witness something in these lower states, my spirit helper would neutralize these vibrations in some way. On most of these dull astral planes I am invisible to the people there.

The lower realms are quite Earth-like. There are cities, towns, villages, etc., which seem to be replicas of existing localities on Earth, and sometimes the conditions are similar to those on Earth. They are quite "solid" when the spirit body assumes the same wavelength.

In The Silver Birch Book of Questions & Answers by Stan A. Ballard and Roger Green, the spirit teacher replies to a question about greed and power and whether they exist in the spirit world. This was the reply:

10. Greed and desire for power exist

Greed and power still exist in what may be called the lower astral realms. What you must realise is that spiritually an individual is exactly the same one day after death as he was before it. Our world, unlike yours, is one where thought is reality. What you think is real and substantial.

The trouble is that lust for power and greed chain (them) to earth. Though materially dead, they are spiritually dead as well. They are nearer to your world than they are to us. Unfortunately they can harm those like themselves in your world who are concerned only with greed and power.

## Escape from Hell
## Amazon Reviews

### Hell of our own making! - T.R., Mar. 2019

'Escape from Hell is an apt title. This book describes in detail a number of the lower planes in the spirit world and the horrible beings that inhabit these dark, vile and dismal realms. It is a wake up call for all of us to put 'right' any wrongs before we pass on from this life on earth. Well worth reading!'

### A recommended read for all! – Salsaroo, Jan. 2020

'This book is in many ways the opposite of books such as 'The Secret': the account of 'Antonio' after he died indicates the hellish experiences you can manifest for yourself if you give in to your baser nature and live a cruel, corrupt life.

'More scary than a William Peter Blatty novel, it may be easy to dismiss Antonio's grisly account as fiction, although the author offers supporting evidence in the form of accounts of the baser realms from other sources.

'Furthermore, the basic message is in alignment with the message that we have been given loud and clear from various sources for millennia; live life according to your own conscience as much as you can, and make love, care, kindness, and service your central aim.'

### Wonderfully full of spiritual knowledge - Sam McD, Jan. 2021

'Absolutely beautiful book. Read it twice, loved it. I would love to see this book made into a movie. Strongly recommend, especially if you have unanswered spiritual questions.'

## 5. Fifty Famous Spirits of the Past Speak

# Fifty Famous Spirits of the Past Speak

Published February 2019 – Latest Edition August 2021

## About the book

This book is compiled from various sources, from transcribed "Trance Communications" that date back more than 150 years, to audio spirit recordings which were received via "Direct Voice" during sittings with the medium Leslie Flint. Its purpose is to help encourage people of today to openly and honestly recognize that we are all immortal spirit beings living temporary physical lifetimes; and that how we think, live, the things we do, how we treat each other, how we treat animals, how we treat the planet and the environment, matters. For this is what spirits famous, and equally those unknown to us have, with kindness, compassion and love, for centuries been saying to us. Thousands of spirits who once walked the Earth have always communicated with those of us 'down here' who were receptive to them. In this book I have gathered some of the communications from famous spirits of the past. This, in part, gives us a glimpse back in time, and it also reveals to us what the famous spirits wished and still wish to share with us. In part it is what they want us to know about their current life in the spirit realms, which will of course be our future life, but they also want us to realize the consequences of a lifetime upon Earth lived purely for self, or to the detriment of others. And believe me, there are consequences, because those in spirit life have to face their true self, which in the spirit realms is revealed for all to see. The acceptance and realization that we are eternal beings should be common knowledge in this time. There can be no doubting this. And, personally, I know that in this time, 2024 as I type this, a massive change and awakening is underway upon this planet; and I hope that this book will add further reassurance to those who need it, to know, without any shadow of doubt, that 'death' is simply an exit from one plane of life, as we shift our consciousness to the next, the spirit life. Read and enjoy.

## A Little from the Book

### From: 24. Mohandas Gandhi

In the world there is great poverty and oft-times the poverty is due, not only to ignorance, but also due to personal pride, personal desire for the individual who is in the position to suppress. Often religion, unconsciously sometimes, is at the back of a great deal of the world's unhappiness. Religions become strong and groups of individuals create for themselves great mass of wealth, which is used, not for the poor, not for the underfed, not for the downtrodden, but for the personal aggrandizement of a few, not only outside religion, but inside it.

And where there is great strength in religion, often there is the greatest weakness. Those religions who amass great wealth are oft-times far removed from the truth. I have seen this in so many different ways.

When I was on your side and since I have been here, I have seen through the hearts - into the hearts of many of these people who are in, so-called, high places, in high positions, and they are not concerned with the good of humanity. They are concerned with their personal pride, their personal idea of what they consider to be truth, and oft-times they are far from truth.

From: 11. Frédéric Chopin

If there is life as we know in various aspect of nature, in such as shrubbery, flowers, in trees and in rock formation - if there is life as we know in all nature, there's every reason to believe - and I know - there is a smaller kingdom of smaller people who are undeveloped, but they are nature souls and they are part of nature's plan.

I know some people won't understand this but in my little garden, which is very small, are the spirits, but they are not mischievous or dangerous, you call the Faerie kingdom. My music attracted them a long time ago. They have a great power in nature. And, you know, they work under instruction and they can be used by souls from this side to do certain work.


From 16. Arthur Conan Doyle

You know when I was on your side, I was so often distressed. So often concerned with people who even though opportunity was presented to them, they took little advantage of it, and if they did, even in spite of their nature, they would not willingly accept the truth, the evidence of Spiritualism. Even some of those who took the trouble to read books or perhaps attend meetings quite often, in spite of the fact that they themselves presented obstacles from within themselves, who were presented with evidence which would satisfy any ordinary, intelligent person - they would refute it, or if they did not refute it, they would find an explanation for it. Quite often more wonderful than the actual thing itself. There is such a lot that distresses one.

When one strives to assist and to help people find truth, the extraordinary thing is, that even those who profess to be searchers after truth, invariably by their very nature, build up barriers, so the truth has even more difficulty in making itself known and understood.

### From: 21. Francis of Assisi

There are those in your world who cannot understand the immensity of this tremendous truth, in which we as brothers and sisters go, if not always hand-in-hand, through many existences. But nevertheless, if our hands are not joined in this incarnation or in that, eventually we are so drawn together that we clasp each other in warmth and love to ourselves.

Also:

But I say to you all; the time should surely come when you shall begin to see the great truth the great realization of God's love, when you shall begin to perceive the possibilities of freedom, far beyond your wildest dreams at this moment, when you shall perceive that the power of the spirit, which at one time you would not have thought possible, will become a reality in consequence.

For where there is such love, as is poured to you from the realms of the spirit, nothing is impossible. All the fetters that bind you and the chains can be broken. Do not distress yourselves. Whatever state you may find yourself, whatever the oppression may be that bows your head, whatever load you may carry that makes you feel weakened; know that with love, all things become possible.

### From: 27. Joan of Arc

When the structures erected by the hands of man are less sought, and the inward temple of the soul shall rise up and shine forth in the splendor of its natural beauty, then dark and gloomy indeed will seem the past, and glorious will all feel the present, unfolding to every heart new fountains of light and life everlasting.

Oh! the time is approaching when the men of earth shall feel how closely their interests, their immortal interests, are interwoven with the chain which reaches between the earth and skies. And the links of that chain shall be so commingled as to draw down the spirits of the great in good, the great in wisdom, and the mighty in truth, who have long since passed away, ripened in knowledge, purified in love, elevated in their progression in the eternal spheres of light, and now descending to fulfill their mission on earth.

### From: 28. Amy Johnson

I think the only thing is that, if people understood this truth, realized the realities of it, I think it could help tremendously. But I think the vast majority of people are completely blind to it, they're not interested. They don't want to know. I feel that, in spite of religions, and certainly it seems to me that, often people who should know, don't know. It seems often the blind leading the blind. I don't think people are interested. I think they're more and more materialistically minded.

### Also:

And if you treat animals badly then in some odd way, don't ask me how, but it will eventually reflect upon the individuals, it will reflect upon the human race. This is law, natural law. In other words you cannot escape from natural law, and you're bound to have all these things happen, that distress one so, because man has made it possible.

From 49. Oscar Wilde

Question: Can you tell us some of your life on the other side now, what you're doing?

Well I must admit, it's a relief to be asked to discuss one's life over here, in preference to one's life when on Earth; because in any case my life when on Earth is pretty well-known among the gossip-mongers.

If I were to say to you that my life here is not unlike my life on Earth you would probably be very horrified. But it happens to be perfectly true and I've no regrets about it whatsoever. I'm perfectly happy and perfectly contended and I live a life of delicious sin! But only as the world sees sin; because as the world sees sin, it is no longer sin here to be human and to be natural. But on Earth, to be natural is to be sinful. But over here one can be sinful because it is natural. But the world has strange ideas of sin. I live a natural existence here, and I'm perfectly happy.

And I am still having my plays performed. And I am often called upon to go down into the lower spheres - to help. Strange no doubt you may think that I should be called to lower spheres to help?

Possibly, you might even interpret as well, probably I am more suitable to help people on lower spheres, because I haven't progressed very much myself - but actually, I'm very much in tune with all peoples. My mind, I trust, gives me the entrée, even if my reputation does not.

# Fifty Famous Spirits of the Past Speak

## Amazon Review

### Really Interesting - Lord P, June 2024

'This book was a holiday read for me. I found fascinating the variety of points of view provided by these spirits on the 'Other Side' regarding their post-mortem lives and environment, and the new understandings they had gained about their former lives on Earth. The work undertaken by this author to bring all these reports together in one book from over hundreds of years is very impressive. He argues that the reason why people today remain blind to the reality of spirit life is because for the most part they are stuck on the materialist treadmill earning a living so never delve into their personal existence for its deeper meaning. Numerous of the spirits' contributions refer to having led previous lives as part of their spiritual development, a belief yet to be widely accepted.

'The contents of this book are not patently evidential for survival after death as such, since spirits talking about their eternal lives cannot be fact checked. But what comes through is how the understandings the spirits have regarding the nature of the afterlife are corroborated by their various independent contributions. Here you find communications from actors and actresses you've already heard of; and philosophers, poets, royalty, judges and even a former executioner. The recorded direct-voice evidence given through the medium Leslie Flint I found the most interesting; especially so when references to God (as a male personality), and Jesus as the son of God were at a minimum, making the report largely secular. For me this book was about understanding the nature of the greater reality, which includes a spiritual dimension.

'The only issue where I disagree with this author comes from his optimism that humanity's outlook is rosy with things suddenly getting better in a spiritual sense, probably some time in the period 2024 - 2026. I guess I'm a dyed in the wool pessimist for thinking a high proportion of humans are characterised by baked-in greed and corruption. But this does not undermine the worth of this book to which I gladly give five stars for being simply very interesting!'

# 6. Golden Enlightenment

# Golden Enlightenment

Twenty Year Anniversary Edition

Now Featuring:
60 Q's & A's for Seekers of Spiritual Knowledge, Truth and Wisdom

Published January 2018 – Latest Edition June 2025

## About the book

This twenty year anniversary edition of Golden Enlightenment affords me the opportunity to consider the same fifty questions as the 1998 edition with fresh eyes and a deeper understanding and appreciation of spirit truths. It has also given me the opportunity to include an Appendix with an additional ten questions and answers. The intention behind the earlier editions of this book was to provide readers with easy to follow answers to the sort of questions that most people ask when they first embark upon the quest for spiritual knowledge. However, this new edition, while also being suitable for 'beginners', does go further, and information that readers who already have a degree of spirit knowledge may find that it adds to their personal understanding. In my experience, those people who do seek greater spiritual understanding find that such seeking is a never-ending and exciting journey of discovery. It is a journey that inspires and uplifts them. It is also one which enables them to live a more fulfilling and purposeful life, while granting them an inner certainty in their future as eternal souls. Yet there are answers as to why 'this or that' happens; and guidelines and advice to help us live more spiritually fulfilling lives. Our lives do have meaning and serve a higher purpose; as every reader, if they did not know this already, will soon discover. Readers will find that this book is arranged in question and answer style. This makes it easy to find and read, or read again, the answer to any question of particular interest. Each answer is reasonably complete within itself; so some information, being relevant to more than one answer, may be shared more than once. This, hopefully, will help to reassure readers of its relevance, so that the information is not easily forgotten. Indeed, this is something I encourage, that we constantly remind ourselves that we are eternal beings, so that no matter what we face in life, we remember that we will always have a future. It is up to us to make it a bright and beautiful one. Readers who do not know me and have not read any of my other books may, quite rightly, ask who I am to claim that I can answer such questions as contained within this book. As I detailed in another of my books, I can answer by saying that I am a seeker who for decades (from 1981) has researched the world of psychics and mediums, spiritual philosophy, complementary therapies, and all things associated. During this time I have received many evidential messages via mediums from relatives, friends and guides who reside in the spirit world realms. I have witnessed physical phenomena, and seen the faces of mediums transfigured by overshadowing spirit people. I have also witnessed and experienced spirit surgery and healing with positive results forthcoming. I have also received portraits of spirit guides who are my friends and mentors from the spirit realms – some with names independently verified by other mediums. Furthermore, with my own eyes I have seen spirit people and animals on numerous occasions. I have also sat with mediums in a trance condition and conversed with spirit world guides who have communicated through them. Last but not least I have studied the spirit philosophy and teachings given by many different spirit world communicators and recorded in numerous books. It is because of all that I have experienced I have no hesitation in sharing the contents of this book and stating that I accept it as truth. However, I am claiming no infallibility, I am not perfect nor a living oracle of wisdom. This is my acceptance of truth expressed in answers. As all the wonderful spirit sages say, 'take from it only what feels right for you', and of course, we should all do our own thorough research. Happy reading.

## A Little from the Book

This is Q&A number 10. *Is there anything to be gained by the understanding of survival after death and by the study of spiritual teachings?*

Yes, there is. By understanding the factual truth of survival after 'death', and the knowledge which spiritual teachings bring of eternal life and natural laws, we should feel more encouraged to question every action of our own lives, and thus potentially enhance our spiritual growth and progression.

One way in which we can gain is by learning to judge ourselves and our motives in all we think, say and do. Even an elementary study of spirit teachings gives the seeker the realisation that there is no escape from the consequences of one's own making. This gives us the opportunity to advance as more spiritually enlightened beings than could have been if we had lived life without this knowledge.

Therefore an understanding of spirit or spiritual teachings allows us the chance to make greater advances in our spiritual progression than may otherwise have proven possible.

Hopefully, the realisation that whatever we think, say or do, will ultimately be revealed, will encourage us to be more reasonable in our actions. We can also recognise that through natural spiritual law our good and kindly thoughts, words and actions will always reap a greater 'reward', as we could call it. This can be either in this life, or in our spirit world life, or in a future incarnation, or a mix or all three of these.

Therefore this greater understanding of natural laws should always be considered a blessing. Undoubtedly, it is always better to have knowledge than to be ignorant. It should never be considered a burden, with every action being weighed for or against us. At times we all make mistakes, poor judgements, and take wrong actions; if we were perfect we would have no need to be here.

Hopefully, it should also help us to be more tolerant of others and to be more able to correct our own mistakes. As this understanding becomes more deeply rooted in our conscious thoughts we should, in time, and with practise, find that our actions spontaneously take this reality into account; and when this happens, we are really making spiritual progress.

The study of spiritual teachings should enhance and expand our understanding, bringing to us all the more wisdom and reason for living life with a spiritual outlook. Study provides answers, but at the same time it can create more questions in the mind, which is a good thing, because as we seek-out more answers our understanding can grow.

In the Western world we have mostly been starved of spiritual truth in our upbringing. The so-called truth of the television news relays to us so much negative information; with spiritual knowledge we can understand the positive, starting with the fact that we, and everyone else in the world is immortal, and that nobody has, or ever will, truly die.

By absorbing spiritual teachings we therefore become more aware of our true purpose for living; and this awareness allows us to direct our lives in accordance with natural laws, and the opportunity to progress much further than may prove possible for those who unfortunately, or through lack of desire, are without understanding.

## Golden Enlightenment

### Amazon Reviews

#### Amazing truths about the world of spirituality - Tee Taylor, March 2023

'I picked up this book from my local spiritual centre. I prefer to read books on kindle so I searched and there it was. For free with my membership. So I believe I was led to read. I can only say how enlightening it is to read. I'm a newbie to spiritual things. This answered every question I have or have had in the past. It's very easy to read and is not boring by any means. 10/10 for me.

'He has more books he's written so I'm off to find another. Thanks James. You really are gifted.'

#### A spiritual asset - Tania Sampford, Oct. 2019

'A truly amazing read and an asset to any spiritual reference book collection. Such a unique format and easy to follow, whilst also enhancing spiritual knowledge and awareness. Very highly recommended indeed.'

#### This book is a wonderful celebration of what linking with spirit is all about - R. Edwards, June 2018

'This book is a wonderful celebration of what linking with spirit is all about. It is easy to read and full of excellent explanations of the various aspects of how spirit touch our lives and can contribute to our own progression on our soul pathway. Ray. x'

# 7. Help Yourself to a Better Life

# Help Yourself to a Better Life

A Collation of Writings

Published January 2020 - Latest Edition September 2020

## About the book

This book contains a collection of enlightening material, along with some uplifting humour. Each chapter was once a popular booklet. The chapters cover, "Spiritual Humour", and a revealing question and answer exposé. Then something on the significance of Colour, Crystals and Gemstones. Jumping next to an "Adventures in Consciousness" that includes a true story. The book also includes chapters on "Spiritual healing", and the power of the mind in two chapters titled, "A Healthy Mind" and "A Healthy Mind II", and one that in its own way is associated with the mind titled, "Ancient Fear: Modern Religion".

## A Little from the Book

From the section on 'Positive Thinking'.

Health issues can undoubtedly be caused by negative thinking. Medical surveys have shown that poor mental attitudes and stress can be harmful to the immune system. Unhappiness, fear and any emotion that is negative can disturb our balance both mental and physical, whereas, a cheerful attitude can prove a more effective remedy to sickness than drugs.

Since stress and poor mental attitudes impair the efficiency of the immune system, it is not surprising that they can lead to disease. Poor diets also have an effect but what we eat is often less important than what we allow to eat at us.

In short, to a large degree it is how we think that determines our health or otherwise. The mind is the master of our thoughts and emotions, so albeit unknowingly, it decides how healthy or otherwise we are. When we think, positively or negatively, we not only send out energy, we also absorb energy. If the energy is negative it passes through the system of finer energy bodies, chakras and meridian pathways like an 'off-key' vibration. This, when seen clairvoyantly, has been described as like a dark cloud or mass of energy; with the density being subject to the severity of affect caused by the negative emotion which triggered the 'off-key' vibration.

If the negative energy relates to an emotional or mental situation it will first appear in the appropriate finer energy body, because the finer energy bodies are the initial 'control stations' for all aspects under their influence, our physical, emotional and mental 'big-brothers.' From there any disturbance will be transmitted or transferred, in vibrational code, to all aspects of being. Including the chakras; and then along the meridian pathways to the glands and organs of the physical body. The vibrational 'message' does not stop to think it might harm or damage the physical body.

The effect of negative energy upon the chakras causes them to function less efficiently, they draw in less of the vital spiritual life-force energies from the atmosphere, and appear to spin or vibrate at a reduced speed. Subsequently, a reduced amount of life-force energy is passed along the meridian pathways that, because of the negative energy, can become congested or even blocked, just as fatty substances can congest or block physical veins and arteries. Indeed slower vibrational energy, such as negative energy, does have greater density, so it is quite conceivable that meridian pathways 'designed' for finer (less dense) energy can become blocked by the presence of denser energy.

## Help Yourself to a Better Life
Amazon Reviews

### A great read - Robert Goodwin, Sept. 2016

'James McQuitty is a man of enormous integrity and possess a wealth of spiritual knowledge and understanding of the human condition. His writings and delivered in a down to earth way that appeals to readers young and old, mixing practical solutions with age old wisdom and truth. I recommend this and his other books to anyone seeking to improve their outlook on life and expand their own understanding of this world and what lies beyond.'

### I helped myself when I purchased this, great value - DawnIW, Aug. 2014

'This book contains an amazing collection of material that in different parts is both fun and enlightening to read.'

# 8. How Psychics and Mediums Work, The Spirit & the Aura

# How Psychics and Mediums Work, The Spirit and the Aura

Published March 2014 – Latest Edition July 2025

## About the book

This book is written to help people understand how psychics and mediums work. While it will also help them to understand more about the human spirit and the energies which surround each of us, often referred to as the "aura".

The chapter titles give one a good idea of what is covered within. They are: **1.** How Psychics Work; **2.** How Mediums Work; **3.** From Psychic to Medium; **4.** What we should expect from a psychic; **5.** What we should expect from a medium; **6.** The difficulties mediums encounter and why predictions can fail; **7.** Mediumship: Has Many Expressions; **8.** The Spirit and the Aura.

## A Little from the Book

*This is from chapter 6. The difficulties mediums encounter and why predictions can fail.*

When one thinks of the different "levels" of mediumship I have already covered, I am sure that any reasonable person would be quite surprised to find a medium who did not on at least some occasions encounter difficulties.

Even the better exponents of mediumship are, like all of us, prone to "off days". So it would be surprising to find any that on occasions did not have problems with their reception, and by consequence at least here and there "get things wrong" or make mistakes. The lower their level, the more so; and I mean no disrespect when I say so. We should always remember that mediums are literally attempting to communicate with people who are living in a different dimension of eternal life.

It is to their credit that so many mediums are able to receive and interpret as well as they do. So with this in mind let me summarise and expand upon the difficulties they encounter, and why predictions can fail.

Firstly, to reiterate, we must consider the different levels of mediumship, for these do vary considerably. Some mediums are more naturally sensitive, and many have been psychic or mediumistic from childhood. While others begin to recognise their potential as adults, and from whatever age this happens, gradually develop their sensitivity; and by practise, patience and perseverance, usually through development circles with meditation, enhance their receptivity and learn to interpret the communications they receive.

Even then, if every potential medium were to put all of their spare time into enhancing their sensitivity and learning how best to interpret the often symbolic telepathic communications they receive, quite naturally, some would still be more finely attuned than others.

Symbolic imagery I understand is used by spirit communicators to mediums because of the difficulty of long-drawn messages (it is easier to send the thought of an image than a full sentence). It should also be recognised that thought communications are used quite naturally in the spirit realms between the people there, and their thoughts also convey a fuller meaning.

These days few mediums reach the level of sensitive receptivity required to receive surnames and postal addresses on a regular basis. This is perhaps because there are now just too many distractions put in front of us. Whereas in days prior to TV, computers and mobile phones, and going back still further, to before radio, when there were fewer distractions, by all accounts there were more mediums of the calibre to communicate surnames and postal addresses.

The development of mediumship is rarely achieved without great effort and commitment. No more than it is easy to become a top-level artist, singer, or for that matter furniture maker. I can saw a piece of wood in two but this does not make me a carpenter. I can change a light bulb and an electrical plug but this does not make me an electrician. Very few in this present age are willing to devote their time to a long drawn-out occupational apprenticeship, let alone to one as precarious, and generally with little financial reward, as mediumship.

Some people are natural born mediums; but many others hope to develop their abilities by taking courses. However, people should recognise that no one can develop mediumship without the assistance and cooperation of their guides in spirit life. It is not in the life-plan of some who may be left disappointed; but of course there is no harm trying if one feels drawn to doing so. I could take an art class but I strongly doubt that I would become another Vincent van Gogh or Leonardo da Vinci.

Why do predictions from those in the spiritual realms fail?

Firstly, we must remember that relatives who communicate are often on an elementary level of the astral world. At this level, which we are told is a near replica to the Earth-plane they often know little if any more than the person to whom they are passing a message. Therefore, any prediction, or what a medium perceives as a prediction, is often meaningless.

What can happen is that the relative or friend merely wants to show us that they have been taking an interest in what is happening in our day-to-day life. Or they may wish to make a suggestion, or pass advice as they might have done when upon Earth. They may even be privy to certain events in our life that may appear to be leading to a certain conclusion, and they may say so, either as a misguided prediction or perhaps, and I would like to think more generally, as a forecast of a likely outcome.

However, via some mediums (not all), this may come across as a "sure" prediction. Once again we are dealing with the level, attunement and experience of the medium, and as explained, this can vary greatly.

The medium relaying the message may be under the impression that the prediction is a certainty. Mediums in general have to learn to trust what they receive, to know the difference between a spirit communication and their own imagination, and sometimes this trust may inadvertently encourage them to suggest that such and such a prediction will come to fruition.

Therefore, either because the medium has misunderstood, or indeed because of the communicators desire to believe that what they "foresee" will occur, the message is passed as a sure prediction. But, what the recipient should be receiving is often no more than the opinion of the friend or relative.

Higher guides, our real guides, are far less likely to offer predictions. Especially concerning our physical day-to-day life, for they have total respect for our freewill. So without good reason they will rarely make predictions, for by the very nature of the word, a prediction is most generally a "guess".

Although if we have concerns and ask for guidance, particularly of a spiritual nature, a guide may offer their thoughts or an opinion, but they will leave us to make our own decisions.

Personally, I would not blame an over-zealous spirit relative for trying to give information, whether misunderstood by the medium or wrongly anticipated by themselves. I am sure that they and the mediums endeavour to do their best, but like us, are only human (even if in spirit life). So errors are bound to occur, just as they do upon the Earth-plane, and we, when we receive a message, can also be guilty of misunderstanding or jumping to wrong conclusions.

The bottom line is that life on Earth is our own to live!!

## How Psychics and Mediums Work, The Spirit and the Aura

Amazon Reviews

### An interesting and informative book – mouse, Dec. 2016

'I chose this book because of the keen interest I have in all things spiritual. I think it's well worth a look.'

### Great book, really well written – DawnIW, April 2014

'Good read - explains everything in easy to understand language. Have read many books by this author and am never disappointed.'

### Can't put it down – karlene, May 2016

'Started first few pages. And I'm gonna get in trouble. Can't put it down. Makes it to easy when such an enjoyable easy read.'

# 9. Immortality

## Immortality

A reminder of life's eternal nature

Published July 2017 – Latest Edition August 2020

### About the book

In this book I have taken many of the less pleasant actions and circumstances of earth life, starting with terrorism, war and murder. These, I have put into perspective in relation to spirit facts and eternal life. This, I believe, will help readers to come to terms with, and to some degree raise themselves above, such things. I do not belittle anything, as you will see. However, we are eternal souls, and this we should never forget; and this is why a 'constant reminder' of our immortality, as this book offers readers, can help us in this life.

### A Little from the Book

From: War

*Oh, war, I despise, 'cause it means destruction of innocent lives, war means tears to thousands of mothers eyes, when their sons go to fight, and lose their lives, I said, war, huh good god, why'all, what is it good for, absolutely nothing, say it again...*

*War, it ain't nothing but a heart-breaker, war, friend only to the undertaker, oh, war, it's an enemy to all mankind...*

Lyrics from: War – Edwin Starr

These days, people who start wars do so with the intention to dominate other nations, and sometimes for the sake of their own personal power and greed.

On and off throughout recorded history wars have started and eventually finished.

In ancient times, as today, different reasons or excuses have sometimes been given. Yet all have boiled down to the same underlying motives, a desire to dominate others. This allowing the invaders to help themselves to whatever they find.

In addition, there have also been many battles fought over religion; and yet even these were one group of people trying to dominate others, mind, body and soul, in some cases.

Those with bigger or mightier armies or weapons have, and from time to time continue, to invade certain nations. More often than not lies are told to justify going to war and to cover the true motives. These are shows of physical power.

The use of physical power to dominate and control others is the complete reverse of spiritual power. People, and to degree nations, who engage in such acts that physically, emotionally or mentally harm others, spiritually harm themselves to a far greater extent.

From: Media

The people, all of us, hold the power to share spirit truths, to enlighten all who are willing to listen to the fact that we are immortal beings

*Say you want a revolution, we better get on right away, well you get on your feet, and out on the street, singing power to the people, power to the people, power to the people, power to the people, right on...*

Lyrics from: Power to the People – John Lennon

We do need a friendly spiritual revolution, and it has started to happen. We are very powerful souls; we are the immortals of the ancient Greeks. We are the Gods that many cultures revered and worshipped. Even during those ancient centuries it seems comparatively few people understood that they were the immortals, the Gods, and perhaps in this respect times haven't really changed that much?

*With heart and soul the world is yours, the stars are too, if you bring out the best in you, with heart and soul, whatever you've been wantin' to do, heart and soul will see it through...*

Lyrics from: Heart and Soul<br>– Dusty Springfield and Cilla Black

From: Mental Health

*Happiness, happiness, the greatest gift that I possess, I thank the Lord I've been blessed, with more than my share of happiness...*

Lyrics from: Happiness – Ken Dodd

It is said that happiness is a state of mind. To a large degree I'm sure this is correct. Although, if one is in a state of turmoil, or suffering in practically any way, it is a brave person who smiles and remains constantly happy.

Mental health can, of course, be approached from a number of perspectives. As is recognised, there can be minor through to major degrees of mental health issues.

The stress levels in our world of today seemingly increase year upon year. But one must ask how much of this is down to the individual?

Do people really need to be constantly updated with news of the latest disaster or tragedy as they are billed by the 'oh so negative' media?

The answer is, no, they don't.

I don't suggest that we all 'stick our heads in the sand' and ignore what is happening in the world. But on the other hand none of us need absorb every world 'disaster and tragedy' into our personal energies.

The media encourage people to mull over every bit of negative news, every sad event, every 'disaster and tragedy', every earthquake, every explosion of violence by the spiritually ignorant, until so many people find themselves so entrenched in negativity they slip into a regular state of depression.

For the sake of their mental health and an overall sense of peace it is very, very important for people to keep reminding themselves of the spiritual facts of life. They need to remember or wake up to the realisation that we are all immortal beings. And that we simply can never die – even if we wanted to. It is impossible. The overcoat we call the physical body can perish and eventually be absorbed back to nature, but we, the spirit that provides the power that animates the overcoat, will forever live as the conscious evolved spirit being that each of us will always be.

From: Summary

*Here's a little song I wrote, you might want to sing it note for note, don't worry, be happy, in every life we have some trouble, but when you worry you make it double, don't worry, be happy, don't worry, be happy now...*

Lyrics from: Don't Worry, Be Happy - Bobby McFerrin

## Immortality

## Amazon Reviews

### An interesting read for beginners - Lord P., April 2020

*'As a reader already familiar with the evidence for survival after death, I needed no persuading of this book's main message - that death is not an 'end' involving fearful total annihilation; that instead there is such a thing as 'spirit' and a 'next life'. The book is essentially 'spiritist', with the author assuring us we need to learn lessons about goodness and mutual consideration; the golden rule, you might say. Also, he points out that bad behaviour on Earth can have negative consequences for our personal development in the afterlife. At 122 pages it is short and an easy read. One of its novel features is that the author has collected and used for illustrative purposes the lyrics of over 30 modern songs that reflect the ideas he is talking about in each chapter. The twelve chapters cover such things as the spiritual implications of war, accidents, suicide, getting old and the consequences of negative actions, and more. James McQuitty has endeavoured to make this book positive and uplifting, and I'd say he has achieved that. Personally, I would have liked more emphasis on 'evidence' at the expense of 'lyrics', but then it would have been a different creature and probably not what he intended. This book on immortality will appeal to those considering the philosophy for life that virtually all spiritualists and spiritists already accept. At the end, a suggested reading list covers the work of over 20 authors.'*

### Open – karlene, July 2022

*'I am finding it difficult to write a review where I'm not biased. I love all of his books and find what he says very interesting. Definitely worth a read.'*

# 10. Know Thyself, Be Thyself

# Know Thyself, Be Thyself

Published April 2018 – Latest Edition May 2025

## About the book

This book shows us who we truly are and shares a number of observations to highlight how we can more authentically express our true identity. Inspiring and empowering us to consider where we may benefit from making some positive changes in how we approach life and interact with our families, friends, colleagues, and everyone else we meet in life. Can we live and act with soul awareness? The alternative may well be to follow the flock or to adhere to the expectations of other people; and this may not be in harmony with one's own soul.

## A Little from the Book

From chapter 16. Schools and Teachers:

My friends, other authority figures who may take control over the developing minds of the young are school teachers.

In my opinion, in the UK, English and Mathematics are the sole two academic subjects that by necessity should be taught to children. We all need these to some degree at least.

However, even these are essential only to enable us to read and get by in life. If a child or student should wish to progress further, to write and express themselves in words, or to go into other fields that require a grasp of higher mathematics, then this should be their own decision to make.

Computing is today taught in schools, and no doubt this is appreciated by many children. It wasn't around when I was attending schools back in the 1950's and 1960's. Today many children seem to understand many aspects of this far more than the likes of me. No doubt many have been trained in this field in spirit life pre-birth, but this is a story for another time.

As for modern schooling, it seems to me that in some respects little change has occurred since my school days, when so many children were forced to sit at desks in stuffy box shaped rooms and stare forward at a teacher who much of the time was busy teaching utterly pointless information that totally bored most children.

From my point of view, knowing what I know these days, the single most important teachings that should be presented to every child are the genuine spirit facts of life; these include the law of karma.

Children would then have a far better understanding of what life was really all about. Personally, I think they would greatly appreciate learning about this. Ultimately, of course, it is the single most important aspect to everyone's life.

When I last checked, I found that subjects such as History and Geography are still included in the compulsory national curriculum.

In my opinion, the only History truly worth teaching to children is the bits we could learn from, such as how destructive and indiscriminate war has proven to be. And how numerous world religions have divided people and caused hatred and should be regarded as an insult to the intelligence we call God. If we taught these things we might find children growing-up with greater tolerance for other races and nations.

## From: 21. Doctors and Drugs

It seems that there are still a great many doctors, happy and willing to ridicule complementary therapies or treatments. Does medical training tell them that they can't work? In the same way that it seems many scientists are wrongly taught that spirit communication is a lie?

Homeopathy, herbal or flower remedies, and all similar treatments including the use of colour and crystals, spirit healing and Reiki, are attempts to harmonise the composite whole of mind, body and spirit. We are spirit beings and spirit guides do teach us that disease (or disharmony) appears first in the aura and if left untreated can proceed to materialise in the physical body.

Like orthodox medicine, complementary therapies or treatments are still limited if the root cause of the initial disharmony (or imbalance) remains unresolved. But they can and very often do help – and unlike many drugs, they should cause no adverse side effects.

The average doctor may well shout, "Placebo", or say, "It is a coincidence when a patient improves after having a complementary treatment or therapy".

They could of course say the same thing about their own prescription drugs; and they do sometimes give patients a placebo prescription during their own drug trials.

The physical body is a self-regulating mechanism that when treated with care and respect is capable of healing itself of almost any disease or disharmony. Especially if the mind is free from harmful emotions, such as fear, as the Anita Moorjani case mentioned earlier demonstrates.

# 11. Know Yourself

# Know Yourself

The Real You

Published July 2016 – Latest Edition May 2021

### Please note
Part One of "Know Thyself, Be Thyself"
Includes this manuscript

### About the book

Please be aware that this book more or less contains the same manuscript included as Part One of my book "Know Thyself, Be Thyself" (available through Amazon). This separate volume has been republished for those who solely wish to purchase the easy to read spiritual teachings part of that book. In this book I will help those readers who are unfamiliar with spirit teachings by sharing my understanding based upon decades of research and personal experiences. Because of all that I have experienced and discovered I can confidently state that I accept the spirit information that I have included within this book as truth. In other words, at least as far as I am concerned, it is factual information. It contains no fiction, no make believe, no guesswork and no wishful thinking. Nor is it in any way, shape or form, reliant upon any system of faith, any religion, or religious beliefs or hopes. Happy seeking

## A Little from the Book

### From chapter 12. Earth-bound and Lower Levels:

On occasions those who pass-on can become "Earth-bound" as it is called. Meaning they remain in the immediate atmosphere of the Earth-plane rather than returning home to the spirit realms.

Such people illustrate the fact that life immediately after death is effectively an extension of the physical life.

More commonly, when someone passes-on they are met and guided towards the light of the spirit realms. However, for various reasons some refuse such help and remain close to the physical world.

Sometimes, particularly if a sudden or shock passing, this is because they immediately wish to see one or more of their loved ones on Earth. In fact they may not truly recognise that they have physically died, and may believe that they are dreaming. While in other cases, fear could cause them to reject assistance; for instance a fear of judgement.

Those who remain close to Earth, particularly if they have led any sort of selfish, cruel or embittered lives, may hold lower vibrational energies which have become part of their aura. Such people, and even those who have led quite harmless lives, may also retain what is sometimes called the "Vital" (or lower etheric) body which, under more normal circumstances, quickly dissolves when we return to spirit life.

By remaining attached to the Earth-plane with energies which are of a lower vibration such people can sometimes interfere with things on the material plane and on occasions may even be seen.

If they are malicious or mischievous they tend to be called, "Poltergeists". However, quite often any attachment to Earth is temporary and the personalities intend no harm and may, for example, simply move an object to draw attention to their presence because they wish to be recognised and to say goodbye.

Although there is no literal eternal hell, those who have led cruel or wicked lives may gravitate to lower less desirable hellish levels of the spirit realms until they show genuine remorse and seek to redress the results of their actions through service to others.

At these levels, measuring in Earth time, a personality aspect may remain 'trapped' because of their actions and by their thoughts and feelings, for a great many years.

I do not wish to dwell on this subject other than to say that such hell-like levels do exist. As those who have read Escape from Hell will realise.

Therefore (and sorry if this sounds like a sermon), it would be wise to live a life with respect shown to other people, to ourselves, and indeed to all life, animals and the environment, to ensure we are not drawn down to anywhere near such low vibratory levels.

# 12. My Story

# My Story

## Life Memories, Thoughts & Feelings

Published March 2025 – Latest Edition April 2025

### About the book

Although this book is not a full autobiography, what I have included are 'selected' memories, those that 'came to mind' more readily as I constructed the book. There seemed little purpose in my raking over my long and mostly forgotten memories to include every little detail. Especially, those less than happy ones that we all experience from time to time in life; those of us who live long enough 'down here' most certainly experience both ends of the happy and sad spectrum. The memories I have included do give one a 'flavour' of my life – at least I hope this is the case. So often, people leave little or nothing for those who remain; or for future generations to know them by. I hope readers may enjoy my memories, and my written journey through the decades. As a visual aid, throughout and at the end of the book I have included a number of photographs that I feel may act as either reminders, or a portrayal, of how those mentioned within once looked during their lifetime. I wish all readers happiness. New Earth is Now unfolding, enjoy.

# A Little from the Book

## From the chapter on the 1950s

I cannot say I remember much of the early 1950s. I was born under the Star sign of Sagittarius, in my case, in the early days of December – and on my father's thirty-first birthday! What a gift I was! I perhaps couldn't or shouldn't say for better or worse, but in truth, it is always for better and worse – at different times throughout a lifetime.

Incidentally, my parents were quite likely married later in life than might have been the case due to the Second World War, with my father required to serve in the army, in his case from July 1940 until June 1946 when he was transferred to the reserve. Along the way he was awarded the Africa Star in May 1944 and the Italy Star in 1945. He never shared any stories of whatever experiences he had.

Returning to my story, the house in which I grew up and we, the family, lived, unlike most today, had no central heating, no bathroom, and just the one toilet - and that was located in the back garden – spiders and all.

## From the chapter on the 1990s:

The decade of the 1990s was rather eventful. Quite a few things happened. I left BT in this decade, in 1994 officially, having already purchased a house in Ryde, Isle of Wight, in February 1992.

My initial house was in a turning called Sandcroft Avenue. It was there that I began to write.

I'd had a message (as previously mentioned) from a spirit guide telling me that I should be writing. Interestingly, perhaps, is the fact that I'd had a desire to write way back in the 1970s, and I'd even told my friend John Burton, who naturally asked me what I wanted to write about; my reply was, 'I don't know!'

That, I now realise was the spiritual side of me kicking in, as it were, saying, 'yeah you need to write'. So when I got this message from a guide, who as previously mentioned was speaking through the medium Teena Garton, I began to wonder what I should write about! Eventually, of course, I decided to write a spiritual teaching book.

Even this was inspired by someone I overheard saying that there were no books that easily explained spiritual teachings. So I decided to write a question and answer spiritual teaching book. This (of course) became 'Golden Enlightenment'.

I also wrote a book on religion in the 1990s titled: 'Religion, Man's Insult to God' which was eventually published in the USA. That, again, was inspired by someone in this case saying something rather negative about people who didn't want to join-in saying a ritualised prayer. This prompting me to write and expose and say what I think of religion.

I had to undertake plenty of research for the book, even though I knew that so much in religion is not for the best interests of the people. They're not teaching spiritual knowledge, truth and wisdom, as I subtitled my Golden Enlightenment books. What they're teaching, of course, as most people know, is based on dogma and creed. 'Do this, do that, don't investigate for yourself. Just accept what we tell you'. Sounds like today's government to me! But anyway, I'm digressing too far from my story, so we'll leave that aside. There were more books, especially booklets, in the 1990s. I used to produce them and print them off myself.

# 13. Spiritual Astro-Numerology

## Spiritual Astro-Numerology
## The Complete Guide
## Enabling Readers to Provide Analysis for Self, Family, Friends or Clients

Published June 2013 – Latest Edition August 2021

### About the book

Spiritual Astro-Numerology uses a mixture of Astrology and Numerology. This guide enables the reader to produce an analysis for self, family, friends, or clients, for pleasure or fee. A complete analysis will include 10 Sections.

All you need is each subject's full name at birth (as birth certificate) and their full date of birth.

You are at liberty to adapt, change or add to the information as you see fit (and with my permission if you feel you need it); to reflect your own personality, method of presentation, and awareness.

### A Little from the Book

Please Note:

Much of the wording used in the analysis sections of this guide is phrased in the first person. This enables the analyst to present the information to a subject in a more friendly and personalised tone.

The guide is written more for those who are endeavouring to follow their spiritual nature's rather than those who are pursuing more physical or material pleasures or aspirations. Those following a spiritual pathway are therefore more likely to recognize themselves in their analysis. It does contain generalisations so if you or anyone else come across parts they cannot accept, this is natural. It can happen because we each have free-will and therefore cannot necessarily be pigeonholed, and because some souls are comparatively old and others young. The human personalities with more experienced and progressed souls will be more inclined to follow the inner direction of their higher self. Whereas, personalities embodied by younger souls may be less predictable, and perhaps more wayward in their actions.

There are many ways in which Numerologists' use numbers to glean information. Herein I have selected those I tend to prefer and have many times used. If you investigate elsewhere you will undoubtedly find many other ways of using the numbers. Such information can be added to or replace the information herein so that you can expand your understanding (or usage) to suit your own feelings or intuition and personality.

Foreword:

The purpose of physical incarnation is to enlighten the spirit within, and raise its vibration, so that it might, as it were, be forged and tempered for its next step upon its eternal journey. Existence in physical form represents but a small step upon the never-ending pathway towards enlightenment, as we might call more advanced stages of existence or spiritual evolution.

During the millennium year 2000 I was inspired to formulate Spiritual Astro-Numerology Analysis. This, I hope, will add a little knowledge and foresight to your journey and thus help you in your own quest to move forward and advance.

Since I first started producing my analysis material, quite often in the form of personalised booklets, it has been well received by scores of people. Many of these people commented on the accuracy of the personal analysis I provided for them, and subsequently recommended my services to family and friends. Some also enquired about training in Spiritual Astro-Numerology Analysis, hence the publication of this book – which contains all you need to immediately get started.

If you are toying with the idea of becoming a practitioner in this field, or are simply considering using it for yourself, family and friends, let me assure you that you will find it very easy and straightforward to do so.

Basic maths is perfectly adequate (provided you take care) and you do not need to have a wonderful memory – and I DO NOT recommend trying to memorise anything - I suggest you always look things up in this book – because this vastly reduces any possibility of error.

Have fun...

### Spiritual Astro-Numerology
#### Amazon Reviews
#### Fantastic! – misskerissa, August 2017

Reviewed in the USA. *'This is the best book on numerology that I've read yet! It's comprehensive, provides ample instruction on how to find your numbers and tells you everything from horoscope to soul number!'*

#### Helpful - Dena Shores, Jan. 2017

Reviewed in the USA. *'A very thorough and complete book to do your analysis or start doing someone elses. Great read, will be on my bookshelf for future reference.'*

#### Five Stars - Pat McGinnis, May 2017

Reviewed in the USA. *'Very happy!'*

# 14. The Evolvement of the Soul

# The Evolvement of the Soul

## The Origins and Development of Life

Published February 2017 – Latest Edition August 2020

### About the book

How does spirit justice relate to the animal kingdom? Is a cat, for instance, destined to always remain a cat? Can our feline friends only ever become smarter and brighter and evermore loving and "highly evolved" cats? As a cat lover, and in fact loving all our animal friends, it seemed rather unfair to me if this was the case. These were my thoughts as I "meditated" on the subject. I was thrilled when a sudden understanding or "revelation" came to me. Afterwards, I wondered why I hadn't previously realised what then seemed so blindingly obvious to me. I have since advanced my understanding by adding to what I received. This I am presenting to readers in the chapters of this book. This explains how the human soul evolves. Furthermore, it explains that evolution and progression of spirit is not limited to human life alone; rather it encompasses all life; and this includes the life of my furry feline friends.

### A Little from the Book

#### From chapter 5. The Eternal Journey

Even when we acknowledge the inconceivable amount of time it must have taken for us to become an individualised soul, and this can only be an intellectual recognition, it is still quite impossible for us to imagine the enormity of the eternal journey that still awaits us.

Where will the 'winds of time' blow us?

All we know for sure is that our future journeys will continue along the infinite pathway towards the higher, and still higher, levels (realms or spheres, as they can perhaps more correctly be called) of vibration and consciousness.

By the way, these are not some 'intangible realities' occupied by insubstantial spirit beings. On many, especially the initial realms upon which we shall dwell, the spirit people (and animals, etc.) are as solid to each other upon each level of vibration as we are to each other upon Earth.

As we move forward, passing through each level, we will naturally think and express ourselves in a way that reflects the increased level of soul awareness we shall have attained.

Naturally, no change, not a single one along this eternal pathway, will happen until we are ready to embrace it and have merited the progression.

On our journey in human form alone we may have already undertaken hundreds of incarnations to reach our present level of awareness.

It may yet take us aeons more time and effort, with no shortcuts, to reach who knows what level of awareness?

Will we, when the time comes that we have reached some presently unimaginable height of consciousness, look back, and remember the personality we are today? Will we by then consider this "us" to have been somewhat primitive?

I expect we could, certainly in a comparative sense, but I doubt that those so advanced would think anything but kind thoughts about themselves or anyone else. While we will also recognise the importance of each and every lifetime our soul has experienced.

The immediate stepping stones along the eternal journey have, to some small extent, been identified. Those from higher levels do share certain information with us when they visit those at spirit levels below their own.

As I said earlier, those a little further along the pathway will always reach back. In friendship, love, and kindness they offer guidance, sometimes this is to tell us of possible pitfalls and at other times this is to tell us of the 'glories' and beauty that await us.

Thus we spirit beings encourage each other to continue climbing the spiritual ladder, even if at times it seems a struggle, and that we are stuck on the 'wheel of rebirth'.

There are occasions when teachings cannot be relayed in precise terms; and this is because, sometimes, the concepts are beyond our range of understanding.

When relayed to us such advanced information is often then reduced to a symbolic representation, so that it can be conceived and to some degree, understood.

The next major stepping stone upon our journey will be when we no longer need to return to Earth to experience further physical incarnations. We will then have finished with earthly incarnations (unless we choose to return for a specific reason) and can begin to "climb" towards the higher experiences of spirit world life.

**The Evolvement of the Soul**

Amazon Review

BEHOLD THE TRUTH - Clive A Siegner, Feb. 2017

*'If you want to know the truth about who you really are and what your purpose as a Human Being is, then I suggest you read this book. This book is not long but the Author really knows what he is talking about.'*

## 15. The Great Awakening

# The Great Awakening

## What the Spirit Guides Say

Published March 2023 – Latest Edition March 2023

### About the book

Guides or teachers whose messages are included in the book come from White Feather, White Cloud, Dr Peebles, Sanaya, Jonathan, Zac, Monty, Simeon, Chief Joseph, Jesus, Archangel Michael, White Eagle, Red Cloud and a number of other spirit communicators.

At this time upon Earth a unique worldwide Spiritual Awakening is occurring. At the same time, running side by side with this spiritual awakening, there is another awakening, and it is to the corruption, the greed, and some say evil, that has been and still is rife on this plane of life, but is now being exposed for what it is, so that it can be dismantled and replaced by a more compassionate, kind, loving and fair society.

This book shares information in the form of communications received from a number of spirit guides speaking through fifteen different trance mediums over the course of more than a century, including ten mediums active today.

The spirit guides speak of both the positive impact of the spiritual awakening upon our spiritual nature, which is rising in frequency, and the 'dark agenda' run by 'globalists' or super-rich 'materialists' in cooperation worldwide with politicians controlling governments and directing them to do the bidding of those behind the dark agenda.

This surely is a book that every free thinker should read to understand what is going on both spiritually and to discover how the dark agenda seeks to impose their 'madness' and dominating and controlling agenda upon us all. An agenda that seeks to deny everyone the right of free speech, free movement, and in fact all freedoms that the would-be dictators wish to restrict and control. An agenda that we all need to stand-up to and say, "No"; an agenda we must resist and refuse to comply with. This is a time of revolution, but it must be a peaceful, non-violent revolution. Goodness triumphs through love, non-compliance, and by understanding our true nature as eternal spirit beings; this, the messages within this book inform us, is the way forward.

## A Little from the Book

### From: 1. The Dark Agenda – Part One

The dark agenda of the so-called elite, who are often grouped under the term, "globalists", the "mega-wealthy materialists", has many depths to it. If one truly wishes to delve deeply into this, then many, many books are available concerning "the great reset" or "agenda 2030" and other such labels they give to their dark agenda. They do attempt to dress their plans up as good ideas for the benefit of all and the planet, and they are experts at doing so. But ultimately, if all their plans were successful, the world and most people would find themselves in a dark place. It is for this reason that I believe people need to be aware of certain things. If they are not, then they will be open to the manipulative misdirection and misinformation that is constantly expounded through the media by those with ulterior motives.

These ulterior motives, to be perfectly clear, do not have the best interests of anyone at heart other than the select 'elite' attempting to dominate the lives of everyone else on Earth. Their motivation is based on having, power, money and control over all.

## From: 4. The Dark Agenda – Part Two

Power, Money and Control are absolutely, one-hundred percent what certain people in this world want. They do not care about public health, nor do they care about the climate, pollution, the rainforests or anything else – unless it impacts on their personal lives.

They do not care if their policies hurt the average person in any way, physically, emotionally, or mentally. Nor do they care if their policies cause the premature departure from Earth of the average person. No matter whether such people die from hypothermia, starvation, obesity, suicide, disease, or the side effects of drugs, whether prescription or recreational, or the effects of a genuine or so-called vaccine. Then, of course, there are those who 'die' because of some conflict or war they have caused. And those they have murdered for having the affront to discover a cure for some disease; or find some alternative, more or less, free source of energy. How dare such people expect not to be murdered for trying to help the average person; when those of the dark agenda are raking in billions and billions of pounds or dollars from their current (recommended, by them!) medical treatments and energy sales.

## From: 2: The Great Awakening - What the Spirit Guides Say
## Rudolf Steiner – October 1917
### The Fall of the Spirits of Darkness – Part One

It will be the main concern of these spirits of darkness to bring confusion into the rightful elements which are now spreading on Earth, and need to spread in such a way that the spirits of light can continue to be active in them. They will seek to push these in the wrong direction. I have already spoken of one such wrong direction, which is about as paradoxical as is possible. I have pointed out that while human bodies will develop in such a way that certain spiritualities can find room in them, the materialistic bent, which will spread more and more under the guidance of the spirits of darkness, will work against this and combat it by physical means.

I have told you that the spirits of darkness are going to inspire their human hosts, in whom they will be dwelling, to find a vaccine that will drive all inclination towards spirituality out of people's souls when they are still very young, and this will happen in a roundabout way through the living body. Today, bodies are vaccinated against one thing and another; in future, children will be vaccinated with a substance which it will certainly be possible to produce, and this will make them immune, so that they do not develop foolish inclinations connected with spiritual life - 'foolish' here, of course, in the eyes of materialists.

The whole trend goes in a direction where a way will finally be found to vaccinate bodies so that these bodies will not allow the inclination towards spiritual ideas to develop and all their lives people will believe only in the physical world they perceive with the senses.

People are now vaccinated against consumption, and in the same way they will be vaccinated against any inclination towards spirituality. This is merely to give you a particularly striking example of many things which will come in the near and more distant future in this field - the aim being to bring confusion into the impulses which want to stream down to Earth after the victory of the spirits of light.

The first step must be to throw people's views into confusion, turning their concepts and ideas inside out. This is a serious thing and must be watched with care, for it is part of some highly important elements which will be the background to events now in preparation.

From: 3. Spirit Guides Speak of the Unfolding Age of Aquarius

Red Cloud said 21st June 1935

There shall come upon your Earth plane, through the travail of birth, a new born soul in consciousness and man shall have revealed to him the powers of healing through the mental states of his own conscious mind; man shall heal, for many diverse plans shall be brought about, and Man shall realise through the effect of the many senses which are in him of the power, of the possibility, of the rays which shall come from space, which are held in man's keeping.

He shall work side by side with Angels, not just a few mediums here and there, but every man shall know his kingdom, for man shall know when he passes from the limitations of matter into the Spirit; he shall know how to readjust the law for those in their lowly state of evolution. There will be no need for the physical doctors; I don't mean this unkindly, I am just prophesying for the future generation. For the effect upon man's body he will get down to the cause in his mind, himself, which is perfection already. He will find that the wondrous teaching is true which the Nazarene taught, "Be still and know that I am God."

Where now he suffers from his own mental distraction and confusion at the moment, he will be able to readjust, reveal and recharge the physical at his own bidding.

There will come about in the consciousness a new man; the law of the elements will be adjusted, the physical idea in its crudity, in its suffering will pass, and man shall know he is as he is known, a perfect being.

White Eagle - Revolution or Evolution?

There will be many unexpected happenings in the new age. Miracles, my children, the world will call them. From many quarters a flash of light will come to illumine the darkness of the Earth. The effect will be like a revolution, but not of the kind you think - a revolution of thought and ideas, which are going to flood in before very long.

The truth of the Brotherhood of the ancient wisdom and of the White Light, established long ago, will be re-established on your Earth. Groups will be formed all over the world, and even the governments of the nations will be formed of men and women initiated into the ancient brotherhood of the light of the Son-Daughter of God. The wisdom from the East will be established in the West, to work on the outer planes, on governments, and in the commercial world. It sounds impossible for the spirit of the Son of God to be established in the commercial world, but it will be so. Instead of competition there will be cooperation and brotherhood, and the goodwill which is to come in the Age of Aquarius.

Even the form of governments to which humanity has clung for centuries will die out, and it will be government for all - and not for protecting the rights of a few - by a government under direction from the council chamber of the cosmic hierarchies. This method of guiding and inspiring the leaders of all the nations with the ideal of goodwill, with the ideal of the good in the whole of humanity, is in course of preparation and Will lead to a universal brotherhood of individuals and of nations.

Great changes come. Keep calm, simple and humble, and give from your hearts the truest brotherhood you understand and you will assist not in revolution, but in steady, progressive evolution.

# The Great Awakening
## Amazon Reviews

### Very well put together - Warren James, Nov. 2024

*'The only objection that anyone may put to this book is that they don't agree with what is being said, that they themselves has total faith, trust and belief in the state, their government, the so-called experts who are government funded and that no agenda of any kind exists and that they simply refuse to believe it.*

*'However. No agreeing nor believing does not render the words spoken to be untrue. It's just an opinion. Time will tell!'*

### A rare spiritual gem - Amanda Goodwin, April 2023

*'This is a fabulous book that has been waiting to be written and thankfully the author has skilfully pulled together the requisite information and presented it in a way that is accessible to all who are unafraid to seek out an alternative view to that currently being presented from 'official' sources. Drawing upon knowledge from wise souls in the afterlife, transmitted independently through well-respected trance mediums, some of whom have themselves passed over and several who are still upon the earth, the message is clear - humanity is awakening! Whilst spirit guides and author alike acknowledge the dystopian agenda that is currently upon us, the solution is crystal clear - truth is greater than ignorance and light more powerful than darkness. If mankind is not to fall under the spell of the evil in its midst, then non-compliance, coupled with the raising of consciousness is the way forward. Jim McQuitty points us in the direction of salvation and the wisdom of those whose words he has faithfully transcribed underline the great truth - it is we who hold the aces. We have but to remember what we have forgotten and what has been hidden from us for centuries. A must read!'*

# 16. The Great Awakening-Book Two

# The Great Awakening-Book Two

Further Communications from the Spirit Guides

Published March 2024 – Latest Edition March 2024

## About the book

This book contains further communications from the spirit guides. These were received between February 2023 and January 2024. At this point in time most if not all of us realize that the Light requires no manipulation, no coercive persuasion, no threats to anyone's liberty and God given rights of freedom. The Light simply is. It is and is of, God. We, all of us, you, me, our cats and dogs, all people, all animals, all in nature, are of The Light, of God. We are immortal sovereign spirit beings. How on Earth, or anywhere else in the universe, could anyone believe that those pursuing any dark agenda could ever, for more than just a blip in time, ever hope to 'triumph', if that is what they falsely hoped, over eternal indestructible immortal aspects of God? The war is won, the Light, the good, is triumphant. It could be no other way.

## A Little from the Book

From chapter 1. Stand Up and Speak the Truth:

White Cloud: 'I say to you, my friends, stand up and speak your truth wherever you are or whatever situation you may be in, in the world. Stand up. Be brave and walk your truth in every way that you can. For change in the world, the healing of the world, my friends, will not happen because someone has waited and not taken action. It happens because each one stands for truth and will not sit and wait.

'To do so, my friends, God will put the words in your mouth. God will guide you upon a journey that is of service that will awaken humanity, and where you will join many, many others who also feel the call, who also have awakened, who also are brave and speak the truth, unflinching they speak the truth.'

1st June 2019

<u>Dr. Peebles:</u> 'People are going to be coming together in uprisings and saying, "Enough is enough! We want to celebrate our freedom! We want to celebrate the fact that we are a collective upon the Earth."'

3rd August 2020

<u>Dr. Peebles:</u> 'They're not going to be able to control you, my dear friends; they are really, truly, not in a position to be able to do that anymore. You are in charge of yourself, and that is the part of the awakening that everybody is going through.

'As you move into this greater understanding of love, and the fifth dimension of understanding, you find freedom, and flight of soul. You start to realise that you are not going to have to comply with anything that anyone wants from you.'

11th August 2021

<u>From chapter 2. Overcoming Fear & Darkness:</u>

<u>Dr. Peebles:</u> 'Essentially, the attempt here, to create mass panic, of fear to control the many, rather than the few, is not working. It's back-firing, it's going to create a stronger sense of community than ever before. You are going to know that you need each other upon this school called planet Earth.'

March 2020

<u>Josephus:</u> 'The antidote to this darkness is also being expressed with each day and grows with each day until the light that is focussed upon your world is greater than the darkness that is proliferated on your world. This is the plan,

beloved souls. It respects the free will of men. It respects the Laws of Creation. It respects God's Will, God's desire for humanity to entreat light. So you will come to resolution, beloved souls.

'Although the resistance is great, the ignorance is overwhelming, and the lack of love gives us great distress. Yet, the power of all the elements of your world and our world and God's Will, will win the day, in time.'

27th April 2020

## The Great Awakening-Book Two
Amazon Review

Excellent! – Gayle, May 2024

'Great in-depth look at the Spiritual Awakening of humanity and the Earth! I highly recommend. Very insightful and important for greater understanding.'

# 17. The Reason Why You Were Born

# The Reason Why You Were Born

2014 Edition - Written in the style of an easy to read 'letter to a friend' - Outlining Spiritual Knowledge, Truth and Wisdom

Published January 2014 – Latest Edition March 2024

## About the book

This book is written in the style of an easy to read "Letter to a friend" outlining Spiritual knowledge, truth and wisdom. It has twenty-five sections that not only outline "The Reason Why You Were Born" but also suggest ways in which spiritual knowledge may be applied to one's life. Within this book readers will discover teachings that reveal real and genuine 'spirit facts of life' about our true soul nature, and that these teachings have absolutely nothing to do with any religion. These are facts that apply to not only every person upon this planet, but to all life.

Once found, these spirit teachings enable us to make far greater sense of life. They show us that our lives do have a meaning and serve a higher purpose. Additionally, they shine a light on our future conditions in the spirit realms. It is entirely our own responsibility, by the way in which we conduct and live our earthly lives, as to whether we one day find ourselves in beautiful spirit conditions, or those less desirable.

By reading this book, and wisely applying the teachings to their lives, readers should find themselves enabled to live in greater harmony with the natural spirit laws. Accordingly, they may progress to better spirit life conditions than many find themselves occupying. The choice, of course, is our own to make.

# A Little from the Book

## From chapter 17. Forgiveness:

My friend, our spirit friends encourage us to develop a forgiving nature for a number of reasons. By so doing we release the negative energies which can be generated when we hold emotional states such as anger, hatred and resentment within.

When we hold such feelings within our emotional and mental energy fields (or aura), this can cause disharmony at a physical level of being, leading potentially to disease, as the physical so often responds to how we think.

I can understand that it is far from easy for those who have been subjected to any major trauma in life, such as cruelty and abuse, or for someone who loses a loved one by an act of murder or drunken driving, for example, to be forgiving. At such times it may help to remind one's self that nobody truly 'dies'. Nobody has or ever will.

Spiritual knowledge teaches us that every seeming 'victim' is released to transcend to a higher and far superior state of being; to a level that befits their personal level of progression.

All suffering: physical, emotional or mental, is transient; a blip in time to the eternal soul, but as painful as it may be to us (at the physical level of consciousness), it may be helping to teach a valued lesson to one, or more, souls.

My friend, remember also that no one knows what they may have done in a past lifetime.

We also do not know the pathway that has helped to shape the character of another. Whether it has been one that we might consider reasonably average or normal or one that has seen them enduring who knows what.

You would not wish to be judged for what you did in a previous incarnation. The past cannot be changed, but your future can. No one ever escapes the consequences of universal law. However, for our own sake, we would be well advised not to judge, and whenever possible, to forgive.

## The Reason Why You Were Born
### Amazon Reviews

### Straightforward, honest and informative – Gmax, Jan. 2016

'This book gives one of the most straightforward and clear explanations of spiritual matters that I have ever read and the truth shines out through the words. I have often wanted a book I could recommend to those who are awakening spiritually and who need some good grounding information that's down to earth and without any religious connotations. His style is concise and emanates a loving warmth that is almost tangible. Highly recommended.'

### I have to say I thoroughly enjoyed this book - Geoff Langford, Dec. 2015

'I have to say I thoroughly enjoyed this book. It was well written. No matter whether you are new to Spirit or like me had an interest for the last 10 years or so, there is something of interest for you in this book. It has served to remind me of some of the Spiritualist things I had forgotten and it has also taught me many new things about Spiritualism. It is a book I will be dipping into in the future and on top of that it is a good read. Enjoy.'

### Excellent book! This book is short and to the point - Dave B., Nov. 2015

'Excellent book! This book is short and to the point (just how I like them). 'It covers the topic in sufficient detail to enable the reader to get a clear understanding of why we are here, where we are going, and to help us follow a path that will help our understanding of spirituality during this lifetime.'

# 18. The Wisdom Oracle

# The Wisdom Oracle

## An Aid to Accessing Your Inner or Higher Self Wisdom

Published June 2013 – Latest Edition July 2018

### About the book

Please note that I recommended that dice are used to aid selection with this oracle, preferably two different coloured dice, alternatively, one dice used twice will suffice. (Not supplied).

The objective of this oracle is to help users to access their own inner or higher self wisdom. Within, the author uses proverbs and totem animals as tools to help users to open their minds to greater self-awareness or self-reflective guidance. Readers will find this oracle, which contains 36 different readings, informative and fun to use. Readers may perhaps be interested to know that the "Wisdom Oracle" was inspired by a Chinese spirit guide called Sun Lee.

### A Little from the Book

Dice: 1 & 1
Proverb: Know Thyself
Totem Animal: The Owl
The Spirit of Wisdom

This proverb suggests that you may need to look deep within, at your true feelings, your true motives and desires to check whether they are worthy of the spirit you are. Nobody can know self completely, it is impossible, but connecting with the core of your own being is what this encourages. This is the ultimate call; it is perhaps the most significant throw of the dice possible-the call to "know yourself". It is an appeal for courage, commitment and most importantly honesty; encouraging you to face your true self, your true aspirations, to know self and crucially to be true to self. Yet, as another proverb says, "To err is human". So do not be too critical with yourself if you find shortcomings, for we all have them. If we did not, we would have no need of this incarnation. Another proverb says, "Experience is the mother of wisdom", but this does not come overnight, it is a long-haul assignment of the soul.

The Owl, the spirit of wisdom, is associated with this proverb. It is a wise observation to recognise your own faults and weaknesses, but this alone does not make one wise. Wisdom is to act upon what is found in a positive, constructive and loving way.

Cosmically, we are multi-dimensional beings operating on more than one level of consciousness at a time whether we realise so or not. We are aspects of divinity, aspects of each other. We are individualised aspects of our soul group, which is an aspect of a larger group, which itself is an aspect of a still larger group into infinity, until, by the spiritual law of divine oneness, all is one.

Dice: 6 & 6
Proverb: Everyone loves a good mystery
Totem Animal: The Raven
The Spirit of Secrets, Mystery and Initiation

If your life seems like a mystery do not despair, it is intended that way. The pathways you take are your own choice, they may on occasions lead you away from your lessons but life is a circle, so you will soon find yourself back on the right pathway. This proverb says, enjoy the mysteries that life offers, they are part of the experience. While another proverb says, "Truth is stranger than fiction", so expect many surprises along the way.

The spirit of secrets, mystery and initiation in the form of the Raven is associated with this proverb. The Raven is also known as the trickster, yet is valued as wise in oracles and omens. He (or she) is also considered a messenger and watcher of the gods. Visualise upon this beautiful jet-black bird as you await your own initiation into...well, that is a mystery for you to reveal.

The biggest mystery, as far as most people are concerned, is the meaning of life. Yet, it is so simple; it is soul evolution. Earth (or any other inhabited planet) is used for incarnations. Each successive incarnation presents the soul with another opportunity to progress a little further up the spiritual ladder. We incarnate many times to learn lessons through the experiences we encounter. A final proverb for you to ponder says, 'Those who will enter into paradise must have a good key.' The key is wisdom gained through experience!

### The Wisdom Oracle

Amazon Reviews

<u>Stunningly accurate – DawnIW, July 2013</u>

'*I love this book! Although I have many oracle cards, this book has to be one of my favourites as the readings are so stunningly accurate. I love the pictures and also the idea of rolling the dice. Great value, arrived quickly and recommend it to anyone.*'

# 19. The Trilogy

## The Trilogy
Presenting

The Menno and Mary Spirit Communication Trilogy of Books

This is a book to which I contributed

Published November 2021 – Latest Edition November 2021

## About the book

This three in one book comprises spirit communications, teachings and answers received by "Mary" from "Menno". Menno, when on earth, was Mary's husband. Herein, are his communications to Mary from spirit life, with the help of his own spirit guide. "Oga" - whose spirit portrait is shown on the front cover of this book, was the spirit guide of the medium Dorothy Robins, who also drew the portrait. Oga herself also helped supply answers, as will be found in the third book of this trilogy. I publish this book in dedication to Mary, Menno and Dorothy Robins and their spirit guides, and do so simply because I feel these communications are worthy of continued availability rather than to remain 'out of print' and lost to the world. (I have priced this book moderately because, like all my books, it is sharing that gives me pleasure more than financial gain). I have made a note of just some of the subjects or topics that are mentioned within. These include the Law of Cause and Effect and Karma, Past lives, Reincarnation, Earthbound spirits, Evolution, the effects of vibrations – Sound and Music, Colours, Flowers and Astrology – the planets of the cosmos. Also, Angels, Nature spirits, Devas, and what may sound as though purely Christian – the Trilogy and the Cosmic Christ. I have tried to explain something more about some of these topics in my Appendix at the end of this book.

## A Little from the Book

### Message - Night of August 23rd, 1955

There is much to be said about Astrology, but the difficulty is that there is too much said. In every paper you are told what you should, or should not do, and which is supposed to be written for you. This is not what I mean. There are few great astrologers, and all this is a sort of vague guesswork, because the important thing which is for the most part not remembered, is the exact hour of your birth.

What I indicate is the general influence and power of the Planets. When you have time, I should like you to try to study this as well as you can, for it is a strong Power and not sufficiently realised and studied upon earth.

The planetary rays are vibrational, and vibration is one of the most important things to study, as the whole of creation is based on vibrations. You are influenced by the vibrations of everybody and everything around you, and you have to try to keep your inner peace in order that it will not be affected too much by the proximity of these, so that you yourself are always able to give out good and peaceful vibrations, and fill the things about you with this peace. Control of Power is control of vibrations. Anger and irritability have the power to send out harmful vibrations. Good people take in and give out good vibrations, evil people, evil vibrations, and it is the same with Spirits.

Some vibrations clash and a difference of opinion is apt to bring about a mental explosion which is bad because thoughts create vibrations, good or bad. A powerful speaker is one who not only has the art of speaking, but is able to send out powerful vibrations, which connect with the listeners. Vibration is often being used for healing in your world. I also use it. This is all a tremendous study, and I have only touched on it tonight, but I will try to tell you more about it another time.

When vibration stops, it causes what you call death. This happens to the earth body, but the Spirit vibration, of course, never ceases.

Draw unto yourself all the good vibrations from everything around you - good music, beautiful colours, and so on, and good thoughts too, all of which will add to the strength of your Spiritual Power, and so, protect and seal you off from all bad vibrations.

## Message - Night of August 27th, 1955

You know that when you come over to my world at night, we often go to the Halls of Learning, of which I spoke to you at a sitting some time ago. We choose the part in which the particular thing being taught is of interest to you, and then go in and listen.

It seems as if there one can find teachings about almost anything one wishes to learn, and where questions are answered without one needing to ask them.

This time, you wanted to know more about the influence of the planets, so we chose the Hall in which these things are taught.

The influence of the planets and the zodiac work in conjunction and are very strong, but the influence depends to a certain extent upon the evolution of the person who falls under it.

Young spirits, young in birth and so in evolution, find it less easy to resist certain influences than do older spirits, in fact, they do not realise at all that they should resist and merely think: That is my character, I can't help it.

As Spirits become more evolved through many births, the realisation comes to them why they were born at that time, and what they may accept or resist in these planetary influences, using them as a means of progress and learning. They are then able to study these forces and to learn much from them. Through this study they can better understand their own characters, and be able to carry out an old saying 'Know thyself', which is necessary to the learning of their lesson in each special class of the earth School. Parents should be more careful in noting the exact time of birth of each child.

From: Section VII - The Animal Kingdom

586. Do dogs live in the Spirit World?

The answer is yes, of course they do. Menno says that in your case, your little dog, long since in the Spirit World, immediately re-joined him and has remained with him ever since, and that he often comes to you although you cannot see him.

588. If my little dog, now in the Spirit World, comes back to earth, will he continue to evolve and progress?

Oh yes, individuality once gained cannot be lost, and he will certainly evolve and progress in another earth life.

589. Can dogs go back to earth as human beings?

Yes, higher animals, if they are loved, are given by that love a little of the human Spirit and so may ultimately return in human form.

594. Are there not many human beings who are in evolution far below that of the more evolved animals?

Yes, because man has never understood or realised the closeness between animal and himself.

595. Is it possible for domestic animals and birds to go back to earth as human beings, and if so, how does this come about?

Yes. If they have been taken care of and loved, then part of the Spirit of the man who loves them has gone into the creature. You give to your little bird or dog your love, and if it grows in intelligence and love within the compass of your love, it may become an individual. It is because part of the Spirit of the human being who cares for and loves it, has gone into the creature that this addition has gone toward making it into an individual Spirit. It is the magic of love.

598. Do the higher animals evolve into human beings?

Yes, they do, with the help of the love given them by human beings, and sometimes they evolve into protective beings for others still in the animal kingdom. The Guide shows to Oga a great Spiritual Being, who has evolved from the animal kingdom, and continues to evolve just as all other high beings do.

### The Trilogy

Amazon Review

A REAL GEM – John, June 2024

'All three books contained within a single volume have an aura of genuine and sincere communications with the Spirit world. It is a great service to see that such information is not lost in the past and the book is very well printed by Amazon.

'Like all good books it stimulates further questions and I thoroughly recommend it for seekers of the Truth.'

# The Author

James McQuitty was born in Putney, London in 1950, and worked there for many years before moving to Ryde, Isle of Wight, UK in 1992 where he settled.

He began to seriously study spiritual philosophy in 1981, and at this time he also began to regularly attend demonstrations by the renowned medium Jessie Nason.

Since then he has had many personal experiences and seen spirit visitors on numerous occasions, as well as receiving a great number of spirit communications via other mediums. These include a trance communication message that led to him becoming an author, with the release of his first book in 1994.

In his books he shares an understanding of our true status in this universe, which is that of immortal souls, and much, much more.

His writing style is easy to read and understand, enabling even those who are new to the subjects covered to finish highly informed and greatly inspired.

Email: jamesmcquitty9@proton.me

Robert Goodwin on Facebook:
https://www.facebook.com/robert.goodwin.3914

# Titles No Longer Available

Below are seven of my one time published books that are no longer available - other than perhaps as second-hand copies:

### Golden Enlightenment
A Beginners Handbook for Seekers of
Spiritual Knowledge, Truth and Wisdom – Jan. 1994

### Religion-Man's Insult to God
Revealed: The Hypocrisy of Christianity
& The Truth of Eternal Life - 1997

### Golden Enlightenment II
50+ Answers for Seekers of
Spiritual Knowledge, Truth and Wisdom – Dec. 1998

### Over the Rainbow
Reflecting Light on Psychics, Mediums
And the Spiritual Nature of Life - 2004

**The Search for the Fountain of Enlightenment -** June 2015

**Spirit Art Portraits Collection** – Oct. 2016

**The Spirit World Realms: The Brighter and the Darker Realms and Helping Earthbound Souls -** March 2020

Printed in Dunstable, United Kingdom

66084857R00067